Digital Marketing Secrets for Contractors

7 Steps to Attract More Leads, Close More Sales & Boost Your Revenue—Using Online Advertising That Works!

Matt Thibeau

To my parents, astute mentors, and loving girlfriend: Thank you…

Your support means more than you know.

BONUS OFFER – *Download Your Free Audio Book*

Thank you so much for purchasing your copy of Digital Marketing Secrets for Contractors. If you are anything like me, you are much more of an auditory learner and always on the go. With that in mind, I have also recorded an audio version of this material so you can listen while you drive, work, eat or travel!

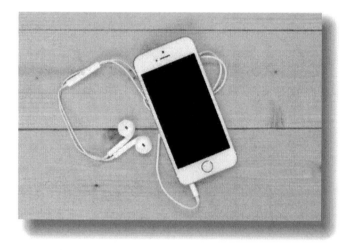

<u>Go to the back of this book</u> for more details on how to download your FREE mp3 audio version of this material!

TABLE OF CONTENTS

Contents

INTRODUCTION: WHY THIS MATTERS

You're a hard-working residential contractor and home improvement renovation expert. You have your own business. And it's been relatively successful.

But lately, you've reached a point in your career where you're wanting to get "off the tools." You feel kind of ... well, *stuck.*

You don't want to be referred to any more as "that reno guy with a truck." And you don't want to have to keep showing up onsite every single day, for every single project.

You want to be able to start hiring more help. To expand your company. To have the time and freedom to focus on other aspects of the business (not to mention your personal life—it would be nice to take a week or two off every so often).

But here's the catch I know you're grappling with …

You know that to achieve all these things, you need a steady flow of new customers. You know, deep down, that referrals just aren't enough to support what you want. You want more options of jobs to choose from. And that means putting effort and investment into marketing.

But … well, you kind of hate marketing.

And this may surprise you but—*I get it.*

I'm a professional marketer myself. And throughout my career, I've worked with countless contractors—honest, always-on-the-go people just like you.

When contractors come to me, they often have all kinds of these awful horror stories.

Like how they paid huge amounts of money to these big fancy marketing firms who promised to build a stable foundation of incoming customers—but didn't deliver on results.

And how they put all their trust in these so-called professionals—and how those "professionals" made everything worse.

So let me be clear: I hear you when you say you feel you've been scammed by marketers.

The good news, though? Not all marketers are the same.

And not all marketing (or advertising) methods are created equal, either.

That's where my 7-Step Marketing Method for contractors comes in…

What's the 7-Step Marketing Method? Put simply, it's a foundational stepping stone that uses tried-and-true digital marketing techniques to build out a system for you that:

✓ Attracts highly qualified leads on demand for your contracting business with ease …

✓ Automates the process so you don't even have to think about marketing anymore if you don't want to …

✓ Provides a stable pillar of incoming business for you—giving you more freedom and control—because once those leads start coming in regularly and you hire more help, you'll become more of a project manager … and less of a technician!

You see, we are talking about *going beyond referrals.*

Because look, referrals are great. They're the easiest way to acquire a new customer. But you can't rely *only* on referrals to get new and ongoing business. You need other sources of revenue too. You need to step *outside* of your existing network if you want to continue to grow.

Some contractors brag about the fact they don't spend money on advertising. But with all due respect, that makes no sense.

Because if you could put $2 into a coin machine and get $3, $5, even $10 back every time—well, why wouldn't you just keep doing that again, and again, and again?

Advertising is only expensive when it doesn't work.

The goal of any marketing campaign is to generate *tangible* results. That means more leads, more sales, and more money in your pocket. The goal isn't to get a bunch of likes on Facebook. It's not to have a pretty website. And not to post memes on social media all day.

That stuff might get you some fame or stroke your ego, but it won't get you rich.

In the end, the goal is always to sell and create a return. When you look at things this way, marketing becomes a lot less of a "creative" process and a lot more of a strategic, predictable, and *scalable* way to inject new profits into your business quickly.

But to do that, you need a behind-the-scenes, ever-working system that ensures prospects can not only easily *find* you—but easily *contact* you on a consistent basis, inquiring about your services:

- ✓ A system that operates at all hours *without* your involvement— that frees up your time to focus on other aspects of your business… So, you can work *on* the business and not *in* it.

✓ A system that—when done *right*—will support you and your family, plus pay your employees really, really well… So you can build a better future for everyone.

✓ A system that attracts clicks—and turns those clicks into actual paying customers predictably… Down to the dollar, and day.

My goal in this material is to give you exactly that.

The 7-Step Marketing Method is a proven, tested, "rinse-and-repeat" system I've developed throughout my career… And it works incredibly well.

But don't just take my word for it—instead, you'll see the results it's brought our amazing clients referenced in the case studies near the end of this material.

And for the first time ever, I'll lay it all out for you on paper—*in plain language*—so anyone in the contracting industry can pick this up and put it to work for their business immediately (that means you!).

In your hands, you now have *everything* you need to start getting new customers online predictably and navigate the online marketing landscape without fail—*nothing held back!*

And once you understand the secrets to effective, strategic, and profitable digital marketing...

You'll have the power to create a wildly successful contracting business—allowing you to create whatever type of lifestyle you desire!

My friend, what would that do for *your* business and *your* quality of life? It would change everything, right?

Of course it would.

No bullsh*t, no fluff. This isn't some drawn-out, boring program stuffed with filler and technical jargon. Nope… This material is simple, but powerful.

You might not always like what I tell you, but it's all true. I promise you.

The reason I reference the information I'm about to share with you as "secrets" is because most other marketers don't want you to understand the *truth* about online marketing …

They hide behind industry jargon and technical capabilities in hopes to confuse, manipulate, and distract you from the truth—so you will continue to pay them month after month without understanding where exactly your money is going.

These secrets are convenient for them, *and bad for you.*

My goal with this program is to change all that for you—and expose you to the truth. And why would I do that?

Three reasons, really:

1) I'm genuinely passionate about my work. I *love* learning, doing, and teaching marketing. There's a certain magic about it that gets me giddy like a child with their favourite toy.

2) I'd like to gain your trust. As an agency owner myself, it's in my best interest to demonstrate I can help you by *actually* helping you. So, when you find yourself in need of marketing help one day, I'll—hopefully—be who you turn to.

3) I hate seeing good people get screwed around. Maybe it was just how I was raised. I'm not sure. But my hope is by equipping you with the knowledge of these secrets, you'll be empowered to make better decisions for yourself and your family—and never be taken advantage of again.

And on that note, there's one last thing I need you to promise me before we go any further.

Please, don't take this lightly either. This is serious. So, please repeat this declaration in your mind, or out loud.

Ready? Here we go …

"I understand the marketing SECRETS I'm about to learn are powerful. I will be ethical, responsible, and never use them for bad, immoral, or evil purposes. I will only use them for the sole intention of providing value to others and making the world a better place."

Got it? Beautiful. Now that my conscious is clear, I'd like to introduce to you to the information in this program. Welcome, to *Digital Marketing Secrets for Contractors*!

Sit back, grab your favourite drink, take some notes, and enjoy the ride…

Your journey begins now.

STEP ONE: POSITION YOURSELF UNIQUELY

How to Catapult Yourself to The Top of Your Market in Record Time & Compel Clients to Chase You (Instead of You Chasing Them!)

Standing out as a residential contractor these days isn't easy. Homeowners are jaded, demanding, and have a lot of options to choose from—including the option to do the job themselves.

But standing out is essential. Especially if you want to start landing more quality jobs and grow your business.

So how do you stand out from the crowd? Better yet, how do you stand out so much that clients are lining up to work with you?

Well, you could do what most contractors do ... which is to slash your rates, YELL louder than your competitors, and/or run countless "giveaway promotions" on social media for attention ...

But that's just being part of the noise.

Instead, I'd like to show you another way. *A different way.* A way that allows you to attract high-value clients and close more jobs without ever again being haggled over price or losing the job to someone $1,000 cheaper ...

By using the power of positioning.

Positioning is the buyer's perception of your brand in relation to your competitors' brands.

Positioning is how your prospects perceive you in their mind compared to everyone else. Marketers and salespeople call this your *Unique Sales Position,* or USP for short. This is a tangible, concrete, value-driven *advantage* you offer over the competition. And when used correctly, a strong USP can mean the difference between a thriving business and a failing one.

If you want to create a highly successful home improvement contracting business and get out of the price game, a USP is a must. It's the foundation for every marketing message and campaign.

This makes attracting more qualified leads easier and closing jobs (regardless of your rates) simpler and faster.

To be clear, a USP isn't a slogan. Slogans are used to create buyer loyalty and identification with your brand. That's not what we're doing here. Instead, we're communicating an advantage (or perceived advantage) you offer over everyone else—by highlighting something *different* about you.

There are many ways to create an effective USP. It can be based on speed, quality, service, price, materials and more. There's no right or wrong type of USP. But it *does* need to provide additional value to your prospects.

In this chapter, you will learn the steps for creating a killer USP for your business …

Secret #1: Define Your Ideal Client

Marketing is kind of like catching fish. Different positioning and USPs will catch a different type of client. So, if you want to develop a strong USP, you need to know WHO you're trying to attract first.

Know who you're selling to. Otherwise, you'll struggle to attract the customers you truly want. Of course, everyone is different. But generally, there are three types of prospects you will encounter in the residential market:

1. The Price Shopper
2. The Value Hunter
3. The High Roller

The Price Shopper

For some people, price is a top priority. Price Shoppers don't have many options financially. So, they're always looking for a bargain. You can often find them scouring through Kijiji, Craigslist, and other similar directories. They are attracted to offers and messaging based around price.

Note: I *highly* recommend you avoid these types of prospects. They usually are the most demanding, and they pay the least amount possible. This makes it difficult for you to grow your business.

The Value Hunter

Consider these people to be the average middle-class family. They've got more disposable income than the Price Shopper, and they've got more options to choose from. Value Hunters want the most bang for their buck. They want value! They are typically attracted to offers related to reliability, quality, and bonuses (like if you throw in a free fireplace with your basement renovation, or offer a free lifetime warranty).

The High Roller

Finally, there's the High Roller. This type of buyer doesn't shop based on price, and they don't necessarily shop based on value either. They want three things at the highest level: service, communication, and quality. Offers based around these aspects are best to attract the High Roller.

Once you have chosen the type of client you want to work with, you will need to have a realistic understanding of their pains, pleasures and desires.

You can't attract a type of buyer you don't understand.

… So, let's do some research first. Here's a simple three-step strategy to help you get a better understanding of your customer:

1. **Go on review websites** like BBB, Houzz and TrustedPros, and study the 1-star and 5-star reviews for other companies in your niche. Make sure they're working with the type of clients you would like to work with, so there's an alignment of positioning.

2. **Study the review feedback.** Take note of 5-10 reviews that were very positive and what the customers liked. Then do the same for the negative reviews, but for what they *didn't* like.

3. **Look for patterns.** By this point, you should begin to see recurring things clients liked and didn't like about working with the company. Write all these points down.

This is the basis for your customer research. Now you have a pretty good understanding of WHO you would like to work with.

Now you must become a specialist in a specific area and choose WHAT you will be an expert at …

Secret #2: Carve Out Your Niche

Most contractors offer a lot of different services. They think that by doing this, they'll attract more clients. I call it the shotgun approach. Basically, you're just throwing stuff out there and hoping something will stick.

This is the wrong way to do things for several reasons.

Many times, having a large variety of services only adds more headaches, project delays, and slows down your overall company growth. Plus, it makes your marketing message generic and weak, and removes the "potency" of it in your ads.

So niche down your services! If you want to become more unique and stand out from the crowd, you must become a specialist. Choose

1-2 services you provide and ONLY focus on promoting and growing that part of your business.

Niching your services is a quick way to develop a strong USP and gain momentum.

Now, when I say this, clients often ask, "But Matt, what if I over-specialize? Won't I lose business because I'll be turning away work?"

Nonsense. In fact, niching your services will bring in more business faster than you might think. That's because it allows you to refine your processes and focus your efforts 10x more.

By niching, you can easily:

- ✓ **Attract ideal clients faster**—because specialists exude more authority ...

- ✓ **Deliver better results**—because your delivery process is more refined ...

- ✓ **Acquire more referrals**—because of the clarity on what you offer ...

✓ **Dominate your market**—because you're more focused in one area …

It becomes kind of like a never-ending cycle of growth. So, if you don't have a niche yet, I highly advise you do so.

But then the next question becomes, "What niche should I pick?"

It can be hard to pick sometimes, I know. That's why you should ask yourself these questions first:

- What service makes up most of my/our sales volume, and make the most net profit?
- What service do I feel most confident in delivering?
- Which service do I have the most potential to gain a competitive advantage in?

Don't overthink this. You might decide to change your niche later—and that's okay. The market will eventually show you what people respond best to, anyway. Just pick one niche and move forward!

Now you just need an offer to put in front of them to get their attention and stand out more …

Secret #3: Create Your Offer

Most contractors put little to no thought into their offers or promotions. They either don't have one, or the ones they *do* use aren't effective. That's because, basically, all they do is look at what everyone else is offering and then they do the same.

But these offers are either attracting the wrong type of leads, or they're just getting drowned out in everyone else's noise.

Make an offer completely irresistible and in-line with your prospects' desires. Keep in mind who you would like to attract and what type of offers attract them. Different offers attract different types of buyers:

- The Price Shopper is attracted to any type of offer based around price. While I do NOT recommend you target this type of prospect, an example of an offer you could make that would attract them would be something like:

"Lowest prices, guaranteed. In fact, if you get a legitimate quote for the same job that's lower than ours, we'll match it— no questions asked!"

- The Value Hunter is willing to pay more for better value. That means all your offers will need to communicate they are receiving more in *use-value* than they are paying in *cash-value*. Here's an example of an offer that would attract them:

"For a limited time, we're offering a Free Lifetime Warranty on all our workmanship!"

- And finally, the High Roller wants service, quality, and communication. Your types of offers will be similar to offers for Value Hunters in the sense they're based around quality and reliability. But you must present your offer in a way that exudes more exclusivity and prestige:

"We guarantee your renovation will be of the highest quality. All our materials are sourced from the finest suppliers in Germany, and we offer a free industry-exclusive Lifetime Warranty on parts and labor at no additional cost!"

While the offers you make will differ based on the type of prospect you're speaking to, the principles for making amazing offers will always be the same.

Here are some specific tips on how you can make your offers more powerful and increase response rates, no matter who you are targeting:

- ✓ **Use the word FREE.** The word "free" will always get people's attention. It's one of the most powerful words you can use in advertising. Just remember to make it clear there are no obligations (e.g., if you offer "free estimates"), and you actually deliver on your promises (e.g., if you offer a "free lifetime warranty"). No one likes the old bait-and-switch.

- ✓ **Make your offer relevant.** Don't give away tickets to a sports game or music concert. Not everyone will care about that. The only thing you know for sure is your prospects have some level of interest in your service. So, make the offer related to what you sell, or at least complementary in some way. No random stuff.

- ✓ **Involve scarcity.** Include a deadline or notice of when the offer will expire. If there is no expiry date, put emphasis on a limited number of bookings you can take on. Don't lie about this, though. Be genuine but also be clear you have a limited number of spots available.

✓ **Make it seem *almost* unbelievable.** The offer should seem almost too good to be true. This will grab their attention. Then back up your claims with great testimonials and proof. The closer you can come to achieving this, the better the response you'll get.

✓ **Reduce their risk.** The less risk that prospects perceive on their end, the better. Stack the cards in their favor. Put all the risk on you if possible. And make sure you tell them that.

✓ **Make a guarantee.** Guarantees are a great tool to use in your irresistible offer because they reduce risk and increase certainty for the prospect. Especially if you're willing to put your money where your mouth is. And of course, remember to always honor your promises and offer something of real value.

ACTION STEPS

Create your Unique Sales Position (USP) by doing the following:

1) **Figure out your ideal client**. Do some research to understand their "type."
2) **Identify 1-2 specialty services you offer to your ideal client**. In what niche will you focus your efforts? You decide.
3) **Make an irresistible offer.** Be strategic in your wording so it speaks directly to the needs of your ideal client.

STEP TWO: COLLECT REVIEWS & TESTIMONIALS

The No-Lose Principles to Easily & Ethically Command an Endless Supply Of 5-Star Reviews so You Can Gain Trust Faster & Sell BIG Jobs Without Fail!

Before you eat at a restaurant, watch a movie, or buy something online, you check the reviews. Right?

Your online reputation matters. Unfortunately, too often, contractors will ignore their online reputation. Because of neglect, ignorance, or downright stubbornness, many of them end up with a bunch of bad reviews—or have no reviews at all. Both scenarios are damaging to your business and here's why …

Consumers depend on reviews to make better decisions. We trust the opinions of others. And if most of the feedback is positive or negative, we tend to believe it. Even if we never have worked with that company before.

Think about the last time you bought something on Amazon—or if you've ever been stuck deciding between two similar products. You don't have a personal relationship with either of the sellers. You're also not very well educated on the differences between the products.

So how do you choose between them?

You start to read the reviews. Don't you? And you see what other people are saying about *their* experience.

Well, whether you like it or not, prospects are doing the exact same thing with your business: they're looking for and reading reviews about you.

People trust the opinions of others!

When other people tout your business, that's called 3rd-party validation. That kind of validation is so powerful that all it takes is one or two reviews to sway a customer's decision.

After all, a study in Podium[1] shows that 93% of consumers say online reviews impact their purchasing decisions.

Therefore, reviews matter. They are a critical part in the buying process, especially online. So, don't ignore reviews. Instead, *embrace* them.

This is especially true when it comes to advertising to cold prospects (people who don't know you)—mostly because it's hard to build trust online.

Maybe you're the type of person who has a great personality. Or you go above and beyond for many of your clients. It can be hard to convey that through a website.

That's where amazing reviews and other "trust signals" come into play.

---

[1] You can read the article here: https://www.podium.com/resources/podium-state-of-online-reviews/

But getting quality reviews can be hard. You're busy enough, focusing on getting the job done right. Clients can sometimes be difficult to pin down and get a review from. And unfortunately, once they *do* leave you a review, many times it doesn't carry the impact you hoped for. Like they don't go into detail or mention what you had hoped they would.

If you've received lackluster reviews before, I know this can be very frustrating. But reviews are a necessity in today's world. So, you must learn to master them. Otherwise, you're at the mercy of these review platforms!

Secret #4: Focus on One Platform

There are so many online platforms to choose from for displaying reviews. You might be worried about choosing the right one. Plus, you don't want to overwhelm your clients by asking too much of them either.

People are very busy. So, it can be a lot to ask them to review you on multiple websites at once. Luckily, there's a simple way to go about this. And it's not rocket science either.

Focus on one platform at a time. Don't overwhelm yourself trying to build up multiple review platforms at once. If you're just getting started, I recommend you first start with getting more reviews on your Google My Business (GMB) listing.

Why start with GMB? Mostly because when people search for you on Google, that listing will be the first thing they see. (If you don't know what a GMB is, don't worry: we talk about this later in another chapter.)

If your GMB already has a bunch of great 5-star reviews, focus on another platform and start building that up too. Consider each platform to be "proof assets" for your business. You want to slowly build up as many of these assets as you can over time.

Some of my favorite (Canadian) platforms to collect and display reviews on are:

- BBB
- Trusted Pros
- Houzz
- HomeStars

Imagine a potential client who Googles your company name to do some more research on you (which they absolutely will do). The more platforms your business is on, the more glowing reviews you can have across the board—and the more they will see. These reviews signal to the prospect, "This is a trustworthy company."

Another advantage worth mentioning is you can also display badges from these sites on your website—basically, small icons that indicate you're a member. This helps with building more trust through association.

After all, many homeowners still trust these websites and use them daily. They rely on them to know which companies are safe to work with—and which aren't.

So, show them you're associated with those websites and build up your reputation. Then reap the benefits. It's really that simple.

Secret #5: Timing is Everything

Too often, contractors ask customers for reviews at the wrong time. They'll send an email weeks after the job was completed. Or they'll ask for a review a year later, when they realize they need more reviews because they got a bad one.

Don't do this. Instead, be more strategic with your timing.

Ask your clients for a testimonial only when they're happy and excited.

I recommend you only ask for reviews when your clients are in a pique state of excitement. That usually means the moment you reveal the finished product to them.

This way, you get the WOW effect from them. And this is the perfect time for you to ask for a review. But why is this?

Because humans are *emotional*. Our emotions dictate our words and actions. Our emotions carry energy—and we can feel energy off one another, whether we're aware of it consciously or not.

If you ask for a testimonial at the wrong time, that energy just won't be there. So the ask must be done at the right time. This is the difference between a good review, and a GREAT one.

Think about when you bought your first car. What was your energy like that day? I bet you could barely contain yourself with excitement.

Now, think about how you felt two months later. Sure, you were still excited to have it, but that wow factor was gone. Right? You got used to the feeling of driving the car around, and your initial state of excitement slowly began to fade.

Your clients are similar. When you deliver results, there is a window of opportunity to grab their initial excitement.

So, capitalize on the opportunity when it strikes and ask them then. Not a month after the job is done, when they've cooled off already— but when you're feeling that excited energy they have for your company.

Here's an example of the difference that energy can make in your reviews:

Exhibit A:

"Working with Bob was great. His attention to detail, communication, and knowledge were also good. In the end, we now have the kitchen we always wanted. I would recommend him to anyone."

Exhibit B:

"AMAZING! What a great experience from the start. Bob is a master at his craft, that's for sure! He took care of us from the very beginning and was always there to answer questions when we needed him. We're SO happy with our new kitchen. I can't stop looking at it! If you need a reliable renovations company, he's your man!!"

Obviously, that's an exaggerated example. And not everyone will be as enthusiastic. But do you notice how much more excitement and energy comes from Exhibit B? That's the difference that timing can make—because there's emotion behind it.

Always be aware of your clients' emotional state before you ask for a review. These types of projects usually take weeks to complete, sometimes months so you can get to know your client a bit before making the ask. Yes, it takes a bit more planning, but the result will be much better for you. Go for it!

Secret #6: Make it Easy

Many contractors will ask their clients, "Hey, could you leave us a review on Google?" However, they struggle to motivate their clients to get around to it and act. Even after they *tell you* they'll do it. Why does this happen?

It's not that they don't like you; people are just very busy these days. They forget things all the time. If you're counting on them to jump through hoops to do you a favor, it's not going to happen.

Not only do customers have to go out of their way to find you online, but then they must *write* the review. And believe it or not, this can sometimes take up to an hour for some people. Today, that's just too much time for most. We live in a world of distractions. So many things are competing for our time, energy and attention. So how can you combat this?

Make it as easy as possible for them to leave you a review.

Start by removing as many "steps" as possible in the review process and simplify the process for them as much as you can. Imagine your client only has 30 seconds to leave you a review. How fast and easy can you make this process for them to complete?

The faster and easier to do so, the better. Here are some basic strategies to make the review process easier for your clients:

- ✓ **Send them a direct link** to your review account via email or text message. Whatever platform you want them to review you on, remember to give them a direct URL to it. Now they don't have to search for you. They can just click on the link and go.

- ✓ **Transcribe the review for them**. Get them to say a statement about your company (in person or on the phone), then write it up *for* them. Ask them if you can email over the statement for their approval and possible edits. Once they approve it, you can use the review. This eliminates the need for them to think of what they should write.

- ✓ **Ask them specific questions.** Many times, clients just won't know what to say. In that case, ask them questions like, "What was your favorite part about working with us?" This makes it easier for them to give an answer. You can use that answer as a testimonial.

- ✓ **Bring a device with you for them to use.** A great strategy is to bring a tablet with you to the job site. After you complete the job and they agree to give you a review, hand the client your device (already set to your preferred platform). This makes it easier for them to give you a review on the spot.

There are lots of ways you can make it easier for your clients to review you. There are even software tools that attempt to automate this process for you.

But I've found these are the most effective and ethical means to do so. Regardless of which method you choose to implement, the principle is the same: make it as easy as possible for them to act.

Secret #7: Focus on Transformations

It's important that you let your clients know *what* you'd like them to focus on in your review or testimonial. We already talked about asking at the right time and making it easy for them. But sometimes they will ask you what they should say. This is very common.

In which case, do this...

Tell them to give you a transformational review. These are very popular in the weight loss industry. You know those ads showing before-and-after pictures of people who lost a bunch of weight? The same applies here.

Basically, a transformational review talks about what life was like *before* working with you, and what it's like *now*.

Facts tell, and stories sell!

Encourage your client to paint a picture of what life was like BEFORE you completed their renovation. What was their average day like at home? Were they able to have friends over? What were their emotions as they moved from room to room, or walked around the outside of their house?

Really get into the details of the pains and struggles they had before eventually hiring you.

Then, get them to shift to NOW. Allow them to explain how you were able to turn everything around for them. Maybe now they're able to host parties and impress their neighbours. Or maybe they just feel a sense of pride in the morning when they see their new kitchen, floors, walls, etc.

Remember, *people buy with their emotions.* Great testimonials tap into people's emotions by painting a picture and telling a story. Stories are extremely powerful because we're taught at a young age to listen to them, and stories naturally bring our guard down.

Above all, be genuine. An honest testimonial expressing true emotions is 10x more powerful than a scripted testimonial will ever be. People trust other people's opinions and they'll trust them even more if your reviews are real and honest.

ACTION STEPS

Get started collecting 5-star customer reviews and testimonials by doing the following:

1. **Choose your platforms wisely.** Start with Google My Business (GMB).
2. **Ask for a testimonial when emotions and energy are high.** The best time to ask for a customer review is that moment you know you've wowed them.
3. **Keep the process simple.** Your customers are busy people. Make it as easy as possible for them to provide a review so it doesn't take up more than 30 seconds on their part.
4. **Ask for transformational reviews.** Ask customers to share their emotional journey from "before" to "after" working with you.

STEP THREE: CRAFT YOUR SALES LANDING PAGE

The ABC Formula to Craft a Simple 1-Page Website That Converts More Leads in One Month Than Most Websites do ALL YEAR!

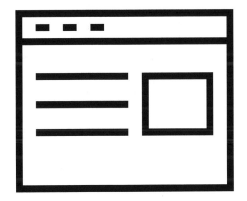

These days, you know having a website is important. I'm sure you have one already. It's more affordable than ever to make one. Website builders like Wix make it easy to create your own website. But not all websites are created the same.

In fact, most websites read like a glorified brochure. Sure, they look good. But do they convert? Probably not. They just look pretty and brag about some of the work you've done.

You work very hard. So, let's make your website work as hard as you do!

If you want to generate more qualified leads, you must use a *landing page.* This is a simple one-page website that's designed to do one thing: generate more quotes.

Landing pages are sales tools. They are specifically designed to build trust, likeability, and authority before you even speak with the prospect in person.

Landing pages also remove distractions. After all, we're talking about only one page. There's no About page, gallery, or blog like on a regular website. A landing page reduces distractions and puts focus on your desired call to action.

Remember …

The fewer options you give them, the more likely they are to do what you want.

Another advantage to using a landing page is you can be more specific. Generalities don't sell services very well. When you become specific, prospects are more attracted to you. This means you can make a specific landing page to sell your niche service.

Finally, tracking results is easy. Websites have a lot of pages and finding good tracking software can be hard (and techy.) Landing pages make it very easy to track results and learn more about buyer behavior.

Okay, so you need a landing page. But how do you create one? Trust me, it's not that hard. There are many drag-and-drop landing page programs you can buy to make this simple. No coding or techy skills needed.

Some of the popular ones I recommend you use are:

- ClickFunnels
- Instapage
- Leadpages
- Unbounce

But truthfully, it doesn't really matter which program you use. They all do the same thing. At the end of the day, what makes a high-converting landing page isn't the program. It's the content and layout on there that counts!

Secret #8: Follow AIDA

Like any sales conversation, the words you communicate dictate the results you get. Provide solutions to the questions and concerns in the prospect's mind, and you'll get the sale. The same goes for the words on your landing page.

When it comes to lead generation, your message is vital for getting people to reach out. Advertisers call this messaging *ad copy*.

Use the A.I.D.A formula. This is a simple, easy-to-remember acronym you can use to structure the layout of content on your landing page to get people to convert:

A = Attention. This is your headline. Pull them in with something exciting and different right at the top of your page. Most people put little to no effort in their headline. But did you know it accounts for 80% of your page's readership?[2]

That means if you write a bad headline, 8/10 people won't even bother looking at the rest of the content on your landing page! So, take the time to write a good one.

Here are 3 key strategies to write killer headlines to stop your prospects DEAD in their tracks:

- ✓ **Write your headline like it's news.** People read headlines that sound newsworthy. Example: *Edmonton Carpet Cleaner Guarantees Your Carpets Will Look, Smell, And Feel Just Like New!*

- ✓ **Include your irresistible offer in your headline.** Remember your USP and irresistible offer? Create a head-turning hook that's impossible to ignore. Example: *Toronto's Finest Hardwood Flooring Experts Offer Free Lifetime Warranty!*

---

[2] To learn more about this stat and ad writing in general, I highly recommend checking out David Ogilvy's book, *Confessions of an Advertising Man.*

✓ **Appeal to their desires and pain points.** Give them what they want and remove what they don't want. A simple headline formula you can use to achieve this is: (Insert Benefit) Without (Insert Pain point). Here's an example, *Now You Can Create Your Dream Home Fast ... Without Spending A Fortune!*

I = Interest. It's not enough to just grab their attention. You must *hold* their interest on your landing page too. This is where your body copy comes in and where you can begin to talk about your services.

However, you must present it in a way that caters only to *them* and *their* needs. Don't brag about yourself and what makes you great. Tell them how you can help them.

Here's how you can quickly build more interest in your message:

✓ **Use the word YOU as often as possible.** Never write about your prospects as "our clients." Talk to them like you would in a conversation. This builds relevancy and creates a stronger bond between you and the prospect. Avoid saying "I" or "we" too much in your copy as well. Make it all about the prospect and what they get out of investing in your business.

✓ **Focus on benefits more than features.** Features are aspects of your service, which could be technical or descriptive. Benefits explain *why* those features matter to your customers. Example: The fact you use a multi-directional floor sander with an integrated vacuum is a feature. However, the *benefit* is a flawless-looking floor in less time without the dust!

✓ **Reassure them and remove pain.** Talk about the positives they will receive and address their pain points. Dive deep into understanding your customer and deepen their interest by removing elements of fear or objection (go back to Secret #1 if you need a refresher on learning about their pain points).

D = Desire. At this point, you've got their attention and their interest. Now you need to build the desire for them to want to speak with you. This usually comes in the form of pictures of your work, and customer testimonials.

But there's a right and wrong way to go about doing this. Don't just throw up any testimonial or picture on your landing page. Take your time here and do it properly.

Here are some general guidelines for building desire on your landing page:

✓ **Show transformational testimonials.** Paint a clear picture how your clients' lives have improved since working with you.

Example: *Before working with Trent, our kitchen was embarrassing. We couldn't have anyone over. Now, it feels like we have friends over every week. We've gotten more compliments than we can count!"*

✓ **Use before/after pictures.** Invest in yourself and hire a photographer to take some professional before-and-after photos. The more dramatic the transformation, the better. Make your "after" pictures bright, and clear to see.

✓ **Keep it relevant.** Keep your testimonials and before/after pictures relevant to your niche and the jobs you want. You will attract leads like the testimonials and pictures you display. So, if you want high-end leads, show only high-end work (same for testimonials).

A = Action. Now that our prospect has intense desire for our services, it's time to command them to act! This is the second most important part of your landing page. Because if you never tell them to do anything, everything we've done up until this point was useless.

In this case, you're going to tell them, "Request Your Free Quote Today"—and get them to contact you.

Now, at the bottom of the page you should have a form they can submit for a free quote. Later in this section, we'll talk more about specific ways they can contact you (form submissions, phone calls, etc.).

But for now, understand *you must tell them what to do here.* This part is simple. But there are some nuances you should keep in mind. Basically, your goal at this point is to make it as easy as possible for them to act. Not only technically, but emotionally too!

Here are some tips keep in your mind when creating your CTA (call to action):

✓ **Command them to contact you.** Be very firm in your tonality in your CTA. Avoid using passive language patterns like, "Feel free to contact us." Be clear. Be authoritative. Tell them exactly what they should do—and to do it right now. Example: *"Call Us Now to Request Your Free Quote."*

✓ **Mention there are no obligations.** People fear being roped into a sales pitch. Make them feel more comfortable about contacting you by telling them there are no obligations associated when you do a quote for them.

✓ **Tell them getting started is easy.** You'd be surprised how many people talk themselves out of acting on something because they perceive it as being difficult. So, reassure them and tell them it's a piece of cake. Example: *"Getting started is easy! Just fill out the form below and our team will be happy to speak with you within 24 hours."*

Secret #9: Pile on The Proof

Unfortunately, it's very easy to fake stuff online. As a result, most people will not inherently trust you at first—especially if they don't know you and you're advertising to them. So you need to prove to them you can be trusted.

This means you must quickly overcome any trust issues and questions they might have. "Who are you? What's your experience? Why should I work with you? Who else has worked with you? What was their experience like?" And on and on ...

You must go above and beyond the typical expectation to display what I call *undeniable proof.* SHOW your prospects you are the real deal. Don't just tell them!

Display proof assets on your landing page. This means showing whatever you can to make your claims undeniable. You're essentially building a case for yourself here. Don't leave anything up to chance. Reassure them through proof that you're the real deal.

Here are some simple tips to add more proof to your landing page and communicate trustworthiness:

✓ **Use video testimonials (and if not, do this instead).** The more senses you engage in your testimonials, the more believable they become. A video testimonial is most effective because it's the hardest to fake. If you can't get video, add pictures of your clients' faces beside the text. The more information you include about the person, the better.

✓ **Sprinkle trust signals throughout the page.** Add various badges to your page that people will recognize and see as credible. As mentioned earlier, websites like BBB, Houzz and TrustedPros offer badges to display on your website to indicate you're one of their members.

✓ **Use original photos.** Avoid using stock images. Not only does it look tacky, but it's too easy to fake. Original, professional-looking pictures are proof of your team, work and equipment. Plus, the prospect's assumption is, "Business must be going well if they can afford professional photos like this. I guess they're in demand, which means they're good at what they do."

Secret #10: Make Communicating Easy

Technology has changed the way we communicate. In the early 2000s, most people would pick up the phone and call someone if they wanted to get in touch with you. However, that is simply not true today.

With the rise of texting, email and instant messaging, prospects have more options to communicate with businesses online. They use these technologies every day with their friends and associates, so they expect you will too.

But here's the problem—most contractors still act like the only means of communication is by phone call. Their websites, social media and other marketing channels most often direct prospects to call them. But what if some people don't want to call you?

Use multiple communication channels. Yes, many people will still call you. Especially if they're more extroverted or in need of urgent assistance. But a large majority would also rather text or email you. Especially people who tend to be more introverted or shy.

If you want to maximize your response and incoming leads, you must open multiple lines of communication for prospects. This means being open to phone calls *as well as* email, SMS messaging, instant messaging and more.

Here are three main communication channels you should have on your landing page to maximize response:

1. **Add a phone number.** Some people want to get in touch with you immediately. Place your phone number on the top of and throughout your landing page. Make sure it's hyperlinked so when people click it on their phone, they instantly call you without dialing. Remember to add a call to action (CTA) with the number saying something like *Call Now.*

2. **Add a submission form.** Some prospects want you to contact them after they fill out a form. Remember to *only* request

information that's necessary (name, phone number, email, and a description of the job they're looking for.) Understand that the more information you ask for upfront, the less likely they will fill out the form. However, the people who *do* respond will be more qualified because there's more effort involved on their part to contact you—which means their desire is high.

3. **Add a live chat box.** Some people want to message and text you to confirm certain things. Do not automate this process with a bot or AI (artificial intelligence) technology. Assign a real person to answer questions through chat. Answer promptly, then coax them into a phone call from there. At *Savant Marketing Agency*, we use Facebook's Messenger chat box option because it's an effective and free way to respond to and interact with prospects.

ACTION STEPS

Create a landing page (essentially, a one-page website) that generates qualified sales leads by taking the following steps:

1. **Be strategic about your content.** Follow the AIDA formula (Attention, Interest, Desire, Action).
2. **Show undeniable proof.** Gain prospects' trust in your business and services using video testimonials, trust signals and original photos.
3. **Make it easy for prospects to contact you.** Provide multiple lines of communication—*not* just phone.

STEP FOUR: MASTER GOOGLE ADS

The Most Dependable, Reliable & Profit-Centred Method to Drive Red-Hot Prospects to Your Landing Page— Instantly!

There are several reasons why you might not be getting as many leads as you'd like. But most of the time, it comes down to not getting enough traffic (website visitors) to your landing page.

To be clear, this section is about how to profitably run traffic from Google Ads to your landing page, not your general website. Afterall, there's no point in paying send people to a website that isn't optimized for sales conversion.

Traffic is everything. But not just *any* type of traffic. Quality traffic! This means people who are interested in what you offer and are willing to act on the offer you make to them.

For most contractors, Google Ads are the fastest, easiest, and most profitable source of traffic, period.

Why? Because people are actively searching for what you offer. Everyone turns to Google to research and find service providers. On top of that, Google Ads allows you to rank #1 virtually overnight. That's a lot of website traffic in very little time!

And unlike other traffic sources like Facebook or Instagram, Google Ads places your ad in front of people who are *already* searching for what you provide. They're not just stumbling upon your ads based on their interests. This makes the quality of your leads dramatically better, and the likelihood they'll convert into actual jobs much more likely.

But here's the problem with Google Ads: most contractors don't understand how they work, or they haven't implemented the foundational steps (like we did earlier in step one, two, and three) to produce the best results possible for their campaign.

Success with Google Ads comes down to many things.

At its core, Google just wants to provide the best, most relevant information to its users. So they rate your ads using Google Ads Quality Score. Your Quality Score is Google's overall rating for your ad.

The higher the rating, the higher your ad will rank and the less money you'll spend. We'll talk more about how to increase your Quality Score later.

I'm not going to get too much into the tactics of telling you exactly which button to push though, because that would date this material. The technology moves so fast and would probably render this information useless in 1-2 years.

Instead, I want you to be able to first understand the foundational principles of Google Ads—because that's what is truly important for your long-term success.

"Give a man a fish and you feed him for a day. Teach him how to fish and you feed him for a lifetime." – Lao Tzu

… And the same applies here. Allow me to reveal to you some of the key principles to running profitable Google Ads, so you can continue to be successful with them regardless of technological changes over time!

Secret #11: Pick Winning Keywords

Success with Google Ads starts with understanding keywords and the psychology behind them. Every day, people are searching stuff on Google. But not all keywords are created the same.

Some keywords are searched very frequently, and some just aren't. Some keywords have *buying behaviors* associated with them, and some don't.

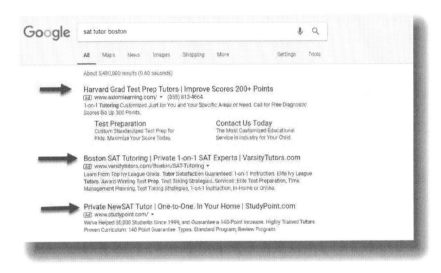

For example, the keyword "Basement Renovations Cost" is considered a valuable keyword if you're a renovation contractor because lots of people search it, and it's associated with *buying behavior*. After all, why else would someone be searching the cost of a basement renovation besides being interested in having one done? Makes sense.

But a keyword like "Basement Renovation Materials" isn't as valuable to you. Mostly because the type of person who would search this is probably looking to do the work themselves. They might even be the competition.

Another example of a less valuable keyword might be "Basement Renovation Ideas." Again, this keyword isn't associated with strong buying behavior. They might be considering a renovation, but they're not looking to hire just yet.

So, why do so many contractors make the mistake of using bad keywords in their Google Ads campaigns?

Because many contractors aren't using data and research to pick their keywords. Instead, they just use their gut feeling. Or even worse, they allow Google's "Smart Campaigns" to do it all for them. (Smart Campaigns are automated ad campaigns built for you by Google's artificial intelligence. While convenient, they use generic copy, broad keywords, and don't include a call to action.)

Going with your gut feeling is a mistake! You need to know exactly which keywords you should choose based off your own research, and carefully select each keyword based on several variables.

I recommend you use a search engine marketing (SEM) research tool. These are software tools that allow you to research specific keywords, and even "spy" on your competitors' winning keywords too.

Moreover, you don't have to guess or rely anymore on Google suggestions that aren't in your best interest (remember, they get paid when someone *clicks* your ad—not when you get a lead).

Currently at *Savant Marketing Agency,* we use a keyword analysis tool called SE Ranking. There are lots of other tools out there. You can just Google "SEM Tool" and find a bunch of options.

However, we have found this one to be most accurate and cost-effective for our needs. The free version works well, but you get limited information in return.

If you are serious about Google Ads, I recommend you upgrade to the premium version.

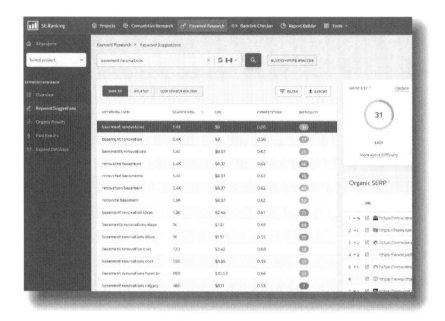

Okay, so now you have a keyword research tool set up. But you need to know how to use it and understand the difference between a bad keyword and a profitable one.

Here are four ways to identify winning keywords for your Google Ads campaign:

1. **Use high-traffic keywords.** The keyword analysis tool you choose will be able to tell you which ones are high traffic (or not). Personally, I only pick keywords that have 1,000+ monthly searches according to SE Ranking. Anything less

doesn't get enough impressions to become profitable. The higher the traffic, the better.

2. **Use keywords with the lowest CPC.** Cost per click (CPC) is how much you're charged when someone clicks your ad. This will vary depending on your niche. Some keywords will cost you $3 per click, while others can cost you up to $25 per click! So, pick keywords you can afford to bid on according to your budget.

3. **Identify negative keywords.** Identify related keywords that you don't want your ad to show up for. Example: words like *salary, job, course* and *cheap* should be among the first keywords to go in your negative keyword list.

4. **Use appropriate matching options.** Google ads uses a matching format for its keywords. At ***Savant Marketing Agency***, we use broad match and broad match-modifier structure for our primary keywords. Your brand ads should always be in phrase match.

I've attached a diagram that breaks down the difference between each matching format, and how Google processes it:

Keyword match type summaries

Match type	Special symbol	Example keyword	Ads may show on searches that contain:	Example searches
Broad match	none	women's hats	Close variations of the keyword, related searches, and other relevant variations. The words in the keyword don't have to be present in a user's search.	• buy ladies hats • women's clothing • women's scarves • winter headwear for women
Broad match modifier	+keyword	+women's +hats	All the terms designated with a + sign (or close variations of those terms) in any order. Close variations include terms with the same meaning. Additional words may appear before, after, or between the terms.	• women's scarves and hats • winter hats for women • hats for stylish ladies
Phrase match	"keyword"	"women's hats"	Matches of the phrase (or close variations of the phrase) with additional words before or after. Close variations include terms with the same meaning.	• blue women's hats • buy hats for women • ladies hats on sale
Exact match	[keyword]	[women's hats]	Exact matches of the term or close variations of that exact term with the same meaning.	• women's hats • ladies hats • hats for women • hats women

Secret #12: Set up Conversion Tracking

Too often, people get caught up in how many clicks or impressions their ads get. But the reality is, clicks don't matter. *Conversions* are the only thing you should be concerned about for your local advertising on Google.

Having your conversion tracking set up properly is key to a profitable campaign.

You can't improve what you don't measure. For most contracting businesses, a *conversion* would be considered someone filling out a submission form, making a phone call, or sending a message through the chat box.

With conversion tracking, you can quickly understand which keywords and ads are profitable, and which are not. It also allows Google's artificial intelligence to optimize for more conversions or lower your cost per acquisition (CPA)—that is, how much it costs you to acquire a lead. This is critical if you want to create a profitable Google Ads campaign!

If you need help setting up anything I reference about Google Ads in this section, refer to https://support.google.com/google-ads. They have everything broken down and explained for you with diagrams and detailed information there.

Now, assuming you already set up Google Analytics, setting up conversions into Google Ads is pretty simple:

1. **Link your Analytics account**—so you can track all your landing page visitors' behaviors

2. **Turn on auto-tagging**—so Google can identify which keyword and ad triggered the conversion

3. **Import Analytics data**—so both Google Ads and Google Analytics can "talk" to each other

Now that you're tracking submission form conversions, you also have to set up tracking for your phone calls. You need to track the phone calls directly from your Google Ads and from your landing page so you can understand which is working better for you.

3rd-Party Call Tracking

Tracking phone calls from your landing page is impossible to do with Google Ads tracking alone. After all, a prospect could just write your number down on a napkin from your landing page and call it later.

You'd never know it was from your Google Ads.

That's why we recommend you use a 3rd-party software to track your landing page calls. Our favorite one is called What Converts.

Basically, this tool allows you to use a tracking phone number on your landing page that redirects to your number—giving you insight on which source the phone calls came from.

Google Call Tracking
Tracking phone calls in Google Ads is, again, pretty simple to set up. Keep in mind though: this tracking will only track calls from your Google Ads, not your landing page.

To set up your Google call tracking, you must add your phone number as an ad extension (see below) for your campaign. Once you do that, set up phone call conversion tracking.

Secret #13: Use Ad Extensions
Ad extensions are additional add-ons to your ad. You know those Call buttons or menu buttons? They're pure gold. Basically, extensions make your ad larger and more robust for the reader to see. They're an easy way to give people more reasons to act directly from your ads.

Extensions increase user engagement with your ads and increase the likelihood that prospects will click them.

And the best part? It doesn't cost you anything extra to enable extensions. You only pay for clicks. Just like on your ads!

There are many types of ad extensions, but I've found a few key ones that are most effective and relevant for contractors. They are:

- ✓ Sitelink extensions
- ✓ Phone call extensions
- ✓ Callout extensions
- ✓ Structured snippet extensions
- ✓ Promotion extensions
- ✓ Location extensions

It doesn't take much time to add extensions. But take your time and complete them properly.

Done right, extensions are a simple yet effective way to gain an upper hand over your competition and take up more real estate in search engine results (mostly because most people either don't know about extensions or don't think they matter).

Remember to go to https://support.google.com/google-ads if you need guidance in specifics to set this up.

Secret #14: Enable Only Search Campaigns

When you're just starting with Google Ads and need to choose a type of campaign, I always recommend beginning with a *search campaign.* Google Search campaigns are ads that show up in Google search results when people are looking for things.

Most contractors are best off running their primary Google Ads campaigns for "search only" because when people need your service, that's where they turn to first.

Display Network ads and 3rd-party network ads—basically, image ads that pop up around the web on various websites—are great for awareness and remarketing campaigns (we will discuss this later).

However, they're ineffective in the beginning of your prospects' journey to buy from you—mostly because display ads are targeting prospects based on their *interests,* whereas search-only ads are targeted to prospects who are *already searching for what you offer.* For this reason, search campaigns are most profitable and effective initially!

Secret #15: Create Action-Oriented Copy

The average contractor doesn't put much thought into the words in their search ad. Maybe they'll use the name of their company and the service they provide. But they usually don't give the prospect a compelling *reason* to click their ad.

Here's the problem: when fewer people click your ad, Google makes each click cost more. The percentage of people who search up a term and click your ad directly after is referred to as your click through rate (CTR).

Your CTR directly impacts your Quality Score on Google and determines your CPC!

The wording above is a fancy way of saying that if not many people are clicking your ad, your Quality Score goes down and increases your costs.

Why is this?

Because Google doesn't like that people aren't clicking your ad. It means your ad is either not helpful, relevant, or functional for the prospect. As a result, your CPC (cost per click) increases.

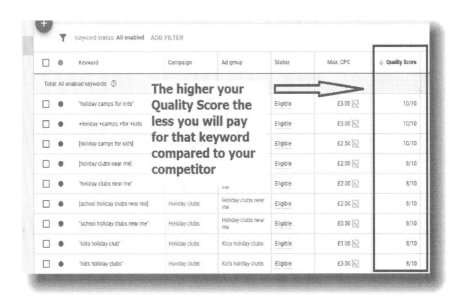

So, if getting a high CTR is key to getting more leads and sales, how do you increase your ad's performance? Well, engagement is key. And one of the best ways to get more engagement on Google text ads is to write copy that pulls them in and makes them want to click *your* ad over everyone else's!

Insert a call to action (CTA) in your ad copy. Tell them what you want them to do. While everyone else is talking about just their service, you put in the command you want them to take.

Your first line in the ad should always be the primary keyword. Let's say it's *Hardwood Floors Vancouver.* But your second line should be your CTA. And in this case, it's to request a free quote.

So, your ad should look something like "Hardwood Floors Vancouver | Request Your Free Quote | ExampleFloors.com."

I know it seems basic and common sense, but you'd be surprised how few people do this (not to mention how well it works). Another thing I like to do to get more attention is place the USP or offer in the ad text.

It would look something like this: "Hardwood Floors Vancouver | Free Lifetime Warranty | ExampleFloors.com."

I recommend you try out multiple ad copy versions (also known in marketing circles as "split-testing") and see which converts best!

Secret #16: Do Google Remarketing

Remarketing is the best way to use the Display Network in your campaigns because it allows you to virtually "follow up" with prospects who didn't convert the first time around. This means you can show different image ads to the prospect, wherever they go on the web.

If you're spending any amount on Google Ads and not remarketing, you're leaving a lot of money on the table!

Here are four advantages to implementing a remarketing campaign:

1. **You've already paid to get prospects to your landing page.** If they don't convert the first time around, follow up with them on Display Networks to get them to convert. Remember, the money is in the follow-up!

2. **The Google Ads display network is all over the internet.** Websites like Forbes, YouTube, eBay, and so on are all included. Imagine being completely omnipresent to your prospects online … *you'll be everywhere.*

3. **Remarketing campaigns are much cheaper than anything else** because you've already identified the IP addresses you'd like to show the ads to. Google doesn't have to do much work … *making it very affordable!*

4. **Your ads remind prospects about your business.** This is where branding comes into play. If your competitors aren't doing this, rest assured you'll be the one people remember!

So, what are the steps to setting up your remarketing campaign in Google Ads? Without getting too technical, it's as easy as one, two, three steps!

(For more information, visit https://support.google.com/analytics or https://support.google.com/google-ads.)

1. **Create your remarketing audience list in Analytics**—so Google knows the audience you intend to target.

2. **Create a new campaign that's specifically for remarketing**—this keeps your campaigns organized and allows you to optimize performance better.

3. **Create your display ads**—so prospects will see them around the web if they don't convert the first time around.

Wait about a week or so for your audience to populate. Once that's done, keep an eye on your campaign and experiment with different ad copy (content) and creative (images) over the next couple weeks.

Google Ads is such a powerful platform. Personally, I prefer it to any other platform because of how much control you have over who sees your ad and when your ad will show. Use the principles I've taught you in this chapter properly, and it could make you a fortune.

ACTION STEPS:

Get started using Google Ads for your landing page by taking these next steps:

1. **Be smart about keyword choice.** Don't just rely on your gut—*research* which keywords are most effective in your niche using a tool like SE Ranking.
2. **Track submission form conversions.** Set up conversion tracking in Google Ads—doing so will help ensure you run profitable campaigns.
3. **Add to your ad—with ad extensions.** They're free and can help you take up more real estate in search engine results.
4. **Start with a search campaign.** Target prospects who are *already* searching for what you offer.
5. **Improve click-through rates with content.** Don't just tell but *command* prospects what you want them to do.
6. **Set up remarketing in Google Ads.** Increase the possibility that prospects who "passed" on you the first time become customers later.

STEP FIVE: DOMINATE LOCAL SEO

How to Flood Your Phone With Local Prospects Searching For Your Services—Without Spending a Dime on Advertising!

Paid advertising is a must if you want to dominate your industry, period. However, once you start getting success with your paid advertising, it's important to simultaneously invest in long-term assets to build stability. That way, you won't always have to rely on just ads to get results.

Enter Local SEO for driving more traffic to your website. Yes, in this section we will be using your main website and not your landing page. That's because we're going to be performing some optimization to your websites search rankings.

Traditional Search Engine Optimization (SEO) focuses on improving your site's visibility in search engine results.

Local SEO, on the other hand, is focused on optimizing your Google My Business (GMB) listing—which is essentially a mini-website that appears in the "Maps" section of Google results for local businesses.

The GMB page is completely free to create and offers a quick snapshot of your company to local prospects. What's even better, though? It's great for lead generation too!

Have you ever typed into Google, "Restaurant near me" or "Shopping mall near me" and gotten results from the Maps section of Google?

If so, you just proved local SEO works.

Your Google My Business page is a local business listing that pops up for keywords that prospects use—every day—to search for and buy from.

So why not capitalize on this opportunity and start getting "free leads" from local maps by optimizing your business listing?

In this chapter, you will learn a simple step-by-step methodology specifically for your business to dominate Local SEO. There might be some overlap of concepts from the last chapter; however, there are a couple key differences to pay close attention to.

Secret #17: Pick Winning Keywords (Again)

Remember that list of keywords you identified using SE Ranking? The same applies here for your website. The only difference is you won't be paying per click. You must outrank your competition on Google Maps. And how do you do that?

Just like Google Ads, Local SEO is mostly about relevance. The more relevant and high-traffic your keywords are, the more likely you are to show up in search results for people searching for those keywords.

Therefore, it's very important to get your keywords right. Otherwise, you'll be ranking for the wrong keywords and you won't get a good return from your investment in Local SEO.

Success with Local SEO keywords comes down to three things:

1. Focus on ranking only for 1-3 keywords related to your niche
2. Pick keywords with high search traffic (using a keyword analysis tool, as discussed in Step 4)
3. Only use keywords with a strong buying intention

Stash this small list of keywords somewhere safe and keep them in your mind. Your job from now on is to optimize all your content online around these specific keywords and the city you service.

Secret #18: Optimize Your Keywords

Although it sounds fancy, the term *keyword optimization* just refers to placing your relevant keywords strategically throughout your online marketing tools.

For now, let's focus on the big ones: your main website and your Google My Business page.

Google My Business (GMB)

Like I mentioned earlier, think of your GMB page as a mini website. It's a snapshot of your business on Google Maps. The cool part is you can edit, update, and customize information on it too. This means you can optimize this listing for your chosen keywords.

If you don't have a GMB page yet, go to https://www.google.com/business to create your Google My Business account and set yourself up with one free of charge. Fill out your GMB info entirely, then complete the following six steps:

1. **Verify your listing.** The first step is verifying your listing through Google's verification procedure. This means you must prove you own your business and the information you provided them is correct. When you're finished, you will see a checkmark and the word "verified" beside your company name.

2. **Be consistent across the board.** Your business name, address and phone number must be accurate and consistent across all platforms on the internet. Also, if you can, use a local phone number instead of a 1-800 number. This tells Google you are a local business in that city.

3. **Use categories.** GMB categories must list services rather than results. List not only your primary service, but also any *secondary* services that you provide. This is where you insert your winning keywords.

4. **Optimize your description.** The description is a short overview of your company. Include all relevant keywords along with your city, website URL, phone number, etc. while still addressing your prospects needs. Use a format like this: "*[Company Name] offers professional [Niche Service Keyword] in [City, Province]. We believe quality, customer service and satisfaction are important requirements to achieve [XYZ Result]. Call [Phone Number] or go to [Website URL] to request your 100% free quote today!*"

5. **Update your hours.** Keep your hours of operation up-to-date and listed consistently across the internet. Include holiday hours and other special hour updates where you can.

6. **Add quality images.** Images will catch your prospects attention on your listing. Do not use stock photos here. Add as many original, high-quality images of your work, team, and branding assets (logos, etc.) as you can. If you want to take it a step further, you can even geocode your images to improve local search consistency using a tool like RoboGeo.com.

Website Optimization

Now it's time to optimize your main website's content to be Local SEO friendly. There are a handful of areas you want to focus on in the beginning stages of Local SEO optimization:

✓ **Website homepage:** The most important part of your homepage is the homepage tagline. This is basically the title of your website. Optimize it for your keywords. This format works well: "*[Niche Service] in [Your City]*".

✓ **Meta description:** This is a short description that touches on your services and ends with a call to action. Try formatting it similarly to: "*[Name of Company] offers top-quality [Niche Service] in [Your City]. Call [Phone Number] for a 100% free quote now!*"

✓ **Headline:** Also known as the H1, your website headline should be clear what you do, and feature your primary keyword. Try this format: *"Professional [Niche Service] in [City, Province]"*.

✓ **Page content:** Now is your opportunity to tell prospects about your business in a Services section. Provide some background information, add your USP, explain your specialty niche, and close with a strong call to action. Remember to optimize each page for your targeted keywords.

Secret #19: Build Citations & Backlinks

With the basics of your Local SEO campaign in place, it's time to move on to developing citations and links. Both will increase your local search rankings.

It comes down to two things:

1. **Citations:** A citation is a listing of your business information (name, address, and phone number) in an online directory. Websites like Facebook, Yelp, Yellow Pages, BBB, Houzz and so on are perfect examples of this. Get your website information on as many of these free submission websites as you can. The goal here is to create a "web" of online

submissions to submit to Google. This will make them trust your business more.

2. **Backlinks:** Ranking high in Google requires having multiple "high-authority" backlinks. This means other credible websites related to your industry have your website link on them. These can be tricky to get. Some of the best ways to get quality backlinks to your website is to appear in guest articles, podcasts, and other online content where you can share your website URL.

Secret #20: Get Reviews

Online reviews play a large role in ranking your GMB for local search results. Mostly because this tells Google you are a legitimate business that helps other people.

In turn, they'll reward you by ranking you higher in their results, because Google wants their users to have the best experience possible.

Use the strategies I taught you earlier in this program to accelerate your Google reviews. Stay consistent, and you will soon have an ongoing flood of 5-star client reviews.

ACTION STEPS:

Get your business on the local map (figuratively and literally) by taking these next steps:

1. **Select strategic keywords.** Pick only one or two to start. Make sure they have high search traffic and strong buying intention.
2. **Optimize for local.** Focus on optimizing your keywords in your Google My Business account and main website.
3. **Get on online directories and other websites.** Having citations and backlinks helps improve your local search rankings.
4. **Promote positive customer reviews on GMB.** Google will reward you with a higher ranking.

STEP SIX: REACH THEIR INBOX

How to Instantly Build Rapport & Get a Big One-Up on Your Competition by Sending Simple Emails—on Autopilot!

Most of the time, prospects will get multiple quotes online from different contractors when they're looking to get a job done. Not because they're just looking for the best price, but to just weigh their options and find the best fit.

The problem many contractors face when landing jobs is, they don't have a systematic approach to "warming up" their leads before they even call them and schedule an appointment.

So right off the bat, they lack consistency in their follow-up. This often leads to deals slipping through contractors' fingers because they're too busy putting out fires, or they just forgot to follow up with a lead.

Without a process for engaging with leads, this can also result in a loss of credibility.

Leveraging the power of email marketing is one of the easiest, most effective ways to indoctrinate new leads in your pipeline.

… Especially when it comes to leads acquired through advertising!

As soon as a prospect requests a free quote through your landing page's (or website's) submission form, they should receive an immediate email confirmation from your company stating you received their quote, and that you will contact them within 24 hours.

Doing this is important for two reasons:

1. By confirming you received their request for a quote, they have a clear understanding of when you'll contact them.

2. Doing so gives you an opportunity to collect their email address for future email campaigns to stimulate repeat customers, or to reengage customers who didn't buy the first time around.

You'd be amazed how much of a difference it makes to just receive a confirmation email with a timeline of when you'll reach out. Most contractors don't do this. And as a result, prospects are left waiting blindly for you to get back to them without knowledge of when they'll receive their quote …

So they begin to look elsewhere.

Imagine if you could create a better experience for your prospects through this process while simultaneously building trust before you even speak to them. Don't you think that would have a positive effect on your rapport with the prospect and your overall sales conversion?

Of course, it would!

Secret #21: Leverage Automation

Okay, so now you're probably thinking, "How am I going to send out a confirmation email every time a lead requests a quote? I'm already busy enough!"

I understand. And that's why you need to leverage the power of automation here.

You need a system that will send your prospect an email confirming their quote, and your response, automatically!

To do this, you need something called an *email autoresponder*. These are email marketing software tools you can buy online or even get started using for free.

Some of my favorite email marketing software are:

- GetResponse
- Constant Contact
- Mailchimp

Personally, we currently use Mailchimp for our private clients at ***Savant Marketing Agency.*** Mostly because the interface is extremely easy to use, and it's free up to a certain number of subscribers.

To get started, go ahead and create an account on one of these platforms and get familiar with it. (YouTube has tons of information to help you do it).

Here is a general three-step breakdown of how this process works when you start using an email autoresponder (for a more detailed process, YouTube should have tons of videos to help you):

1. **Write up a friendly confirmation email through your autoresponder.** Make it clear you received their quote, and that you'll get in touch with them within a specific time frame. This is also a great place to add in pictures of your work and any other content you have (more on this in just a minute).

2. **Integrate your autoresponder with your landing page form.** Most landing page software will directly integrate with the email marketing software I listed above. However, if for whatever reason you're unable to integrate them, I suggest switching email software or use a 3rd-party integration tool like Zapier to create a custom integration.

3. **Prospect receives your confirmation email upon requesting their quote.** If everything is set up properly, your potential client should receive an instant email confirming you got their request.

Secret #22: Keep it Personal

Most companies are too corporate in their tone. Probably because they're trying to come across as more professional. They think this communicates well online but in fact, it doesn't. Not in this context anyway.

Too much professionalism comes off cold, unwelcoming, or phony. You're not yourself when you're *trying* to be. Instead, you're better off being more casual in nature.

So, write up an email that's friendly, concise, and opens a dialogue. You want to create a connection with your readers/prospects.

If you do this properly, *prospects won't think it's automated*. They'll assume it's a live email you personally wrote them because it looks personal. That's what we're trying to do here.

Got it?

Now, here are some quick suggestions to remember when you're writing emails:

- ✓ **Use their first name.** Populate their first name in your email using *merge tags*. This is a great way to personalize your emails.

- ✓ **Refer to them as YOU.** Remember the copywriting lessons I gave you in Step 3? The same applies here. Always speak to your prospects through email as if you were talking with a friend in front of you.

✓ **Use plain email.** Do not add all types of fancy graphics and logos to your emails. This comes off too promotional. Keep it plain white, use minimal branding, and always 12-point black font.

✓ **Sign off using your full name, along with a headshot in your email signature.** Again, you want to present like a person, not a company. You're putting a face behind this computer screen. It's a much more personal approach—and prospects appreciate the transparency.

✓ **Add a P.S. at the bottom of your email.** The P.S. section of an email is the most-read part of any letter. It's good real estate to capitalize on and adds more personality. Here, you can insert a call to action or reiterate important info before your call.

✓ **Use conversational language.** Most people don't talk as formally as they write. Resist the urge to use fancy words and *superfluous* language (see what I did there?). Your vocabulary should be no higher than a grade-3 level when you write-- EVER! (To check for "readability" of your writing, use http://www.hemingwayapp.com—it's free).

But the best way to get the hang of all this is to experience it. For that reason, I'll lay out an example for you. Often, it can be the most subtle things that make all the difference:

Exhibit A

"Dear Valued Customer,

Example Construction has received your request for a quote and a representative will speak with you shortly. Your satisfaction is important to us and we always strive to exceed your expectations in every project we do.

In the meantime, please refer to the following images in our gallery section for your reference: www.ExampleConstruction.com

We appreciate your trust in Example Construction and we look forward to exploring your project soon!

Regards,

LOGO   *Example Construction Team*
Info@ExampleConstruction.com"

Got it? Okay. Now read this one …

Exhibit B

"Hello Dave,

Just wanted to send you this quick email to let you know we received your request for a quote, and I'll call you in the next 24 hours to discuss.

If it's an emergency or you need to reach us for whatever reason before then, just call my assistant Amy at XXX-XXX-XXXX.

In the meantime, you can also have a quick look at some of the awesome projects we've done in the past: www.Example.com

Anyways ... talk soon. Looking forward to seeing how we can help you make your vision a reality!

Sincerely,

Dan Exampleton

P.S. Just reply to this email if there's anything else we should know about your project before giving you a call. Thanks!

 Dan Exampleton
Owner-Operator of Example Construction
Dan@ExampleConstruction.com"

Did you feel the difference? The second example is much more personal than the first one. It just feels different. Notice how I included the prospect's name in the beginning? And used a conversational tone?

These all create a better, more comfortable experience for the reader behind the screen.

I recommend you continue to use this format for *all* your marketing emails going forward. It's proven time and time again to be more effective because it cuts through the noise.

… And you'll always stand out!

Secret #23: Get it Read

You can have the most personal, well-written email ever. But if it doesn't get read, it'll NEVER matter.

Remember how I taught you about the importance of your headlines in Step 3? Well, 80% of readers just read the headline, THEN decide if it's worth their time.

The same thing goes for email. Except it's not the headline anymore: it's the *subject line.* When an email hits your prospects' inbox, the first thing they see is the subject line.

So your subject line better have a compelling reason for them to open it. Otherwise, it's off to the trash bin!

This means you must do *everything* in your power to ensure your emails get delivered. An unopened email means a wasted opportunity. Aim to get a 100% open rate (this can be challenging to achieve in reality due to a number of variables, but it's worth aiming for).

First off, let's talk about email delivery from a technical perspective. Don't worry, I won't get too techy here. But if your emails are always ending up in the spam folder, they're not going to get read.

Here are some strategies to ensure your emails won't be flagged as spam and get blocked:

- ✓ **Have a clear sender address**. It's what appears in the "From" field when someone looks at your email. I recommend avoiding sender addresses that contain lots of numbers or gibberish. Stick to your first name and company name in a format like, *"John from XYZ Renovations"*.

- ✓ **Use a custom domain email address.** Avoid using a @hotmail.com or @gmail.com email address for your email marketing. These are unverified emails and will typically end up in spam. Instead, use a webmail address custom to your domain. Something like John@JohnConstruction.com. These are trusted more than regular emails by email servers. You can buy one on Google Workplace.

- ✓ **Avoid spammy words in your emails.** Email servers scan for words that are likely spam. Avoid using words like *buy*, *sale*, *bonus*, or anything else with a promotional vibe.

- ✓ **Make it easy for people to unsubscribe from your emails.** This one shouldn't be much of a problem as most email software will automatically add an "unsubscribe" link at the bottom anyways. But there should always be an option for people to opt out of your emails at any time.

Now that we've got the basic tech aspects out of the way, let's talk about getting your emails opened using the right words, but first …

Here's how most people separate their email:

1. Junk mail
2. Important mail

The junk email rarely ever gets opened. Especially because it LOOKS like junk mail. Most people don't even waste their time with it. Without looking, you swipe it to the trash folder.

Never to be see again. Right?

But important email ALWAYS gets opened. Because it's important. So just what *is* considered important email? Yep, you guessed it: bills, taxes, work stuff, and finally … mail that looks *personal.*

So personalize your subject lines. Make them stick out like a sore thumb. Position yourself as a friend would, not a solicitor.

Instead of trying to YELL louder than other ads, don't look like an ad at all.

That's how you get your emails read.

Here are some best practices to include in your subject lines to increase open rates:

- ✓ **Use their first name.** Like I mentioned earlier, most software can populate this information using merge tags. Add their first name first-thing in the subject line to grab their attention. They'll want to know what's inside.

- ✓ **Ask a question.** When someone asks you a question, they assume you'll give an answer. Ask an intriguing question in your subject line and you'll be sure to pique their curiosity.

- ✓ **Make it relevant.** If the email is to confirm you received their request for a quote, mention the word QUOTE in the subject line. This sounds like common sense, but you'd be amazed at how "clever" some people try to get. But they shoot themselves in the foot instead. Don't over-complicate things.

In fact, at ***Savant Marketing Agency***, one of the most effective subject lines we use for our clients is: *"[First Name], about your quote?"*

Simple, but it works. Notice how I call them out by their name, mention the word *quote*, AND add a question to elicit their response? It all adds up in the end. There's no point in sending emails if they're not getting read. So, make it count!

ACTION STEPS

Ensure your emails get received and read with these steps:

1. **Automate the process.** Use email marketing software to ensure prospects get an automated response when they ask for a quote.
2. **Personalize your response.** Write an automated response that doesn't sound like a generic email.
3. **Avoid getting caught your response caught in spam filters.** Take measures to ensure your message goes straight to the prospect's inbox, and they'll be compelled to click on it.

STEP SEVEN: SELL ON SOCIAL

The 5-Minute-Per-Day, No-BS Guide to Quickly Building Trust, Credibility & Authority on Social Media—So You Can Get More Customers & Referrals!

You might be using social media right now to market your business, or you may not be. Perhaps you've been posting for a year or two. But you're not seeing the fruits of your labor coming in yet.

Or you rarely post on social media—or not at all. You might not want to post because you're already busy enough and don't want more on your plate. Maybe you're confused or lack clarity on what exactly you should post, where to post it, and how often.

Whatever it is, I know exactly how you feel.

But the truth about social media is it's a great tool for marketing your business. Remodeling, flooring, and landscaping are all extremely visual and work great for social.

Plus, your customers are *already* on social media (like Facebook and Instagram) every day. So, it makes sense to meet them where they're spending time.

Right?

Of course! But it depends on the strategy. Making a post is one thing. But *what* you post is another. And don't get me started on how much bad advice there is out there for social media marketing—especially for contractors. These so-called experts might *think* they're helping you by giving advice, but they're actually *hurting* you.

Because they haven't put their advice to work. It's only theory.

Social media is actually pretty simple. See, there's a difference between *posting* on social media, and marketing/selling your services on it.

Many people cringe at the thought of being too salesy on social. They imagine corny ads with huge discount prices and spamming people's messaging apps. But that's not what I'm talking about here. The type of selling I want you to do is completely different.

Stop thinking about social media as just a way to get more eyeballs on your stuff (for now at least). Instead, shift your focus to building *authority* instead.

Authority is often the missing element when it comes to your social media. Without it, you're basically doomed to play the same game as everyone else. And like we mentioned before, when you do what everyone else is doing, you'll never stand out.

But what exactly *is* authority? Most people imagine a police officer or a communist dictator when I say that. No, that's not what I mean when I say authority.

Authority is the reason people feel compelled to listen, follow and engage with you. They respect you, trust you, and even aspire to be like you. They see you as the defender of your marketplace. A trusted influencer, and a source of knowledge in your field.

Remember when you learned about positioning back in Step #1? Now it's time to communicate your positioning to your prospects. Gaining authority, credibility and attention from your market is critical. But how exactly do you do that—especially when everyone is trying to be an authority (even if they aren't)?

The best way to build authority online is by providing consistent proof to your audience over a long period of time!

It all comes down to proof.

The more proof you can show *why* people should respect you and your company, the more respect you'll get. You must defend your authority at all costs. Otherwise, people will have no reason to follow you.

Proof comes in many different forms, and you will learn all relevant forms of proof for your business in this chapter …

Secret #24: Demonstrate Proof of Knowledge

Knowledge is a level of proof and can build authority fast. When you "know your shit," showing your knowledge can help present you as the expert. Lots of homeowners feel more comfortable working with someone who displays a lot of knowledge about their craft.

But it's also easy to fake, especially online. It's probably the lowest form of proof you could provide. I mean, seriously: how many businesses do you know that have a blog these days sharing *"7 Design Tips to A Better Bathroom Remodel"*?

Most of these blog posts are repurposed content from other similar posts online. So that really doesn't prove you know *anything*. But there are nuances to this concept. It all depends on the *delivery* of the content.

For example, let's say you made a quick (1-3 minutes) video on your smartphone, where you point out a mistake that a previous contractor made—and that you're now fixing for a homeowner.

That would be a strong form of knowledge proof much better than any blog post. Why? Three reasons:

1. **Video engages more senses than writing does.** The more senses you can engage, the more believable your content becomes. On top of that, you're showing your face. Not hiding behind the brand of the company.

2. **You're telling people what NOT to do.** Many times, it's easy to say what to do. But only *true* veterans of their craft will know the small mistakes to look for that only a rookie would make.

3. **The spontaneous nature of the video** (not a high-quality production) makes it seem like you were just on the job as usual and decided to help some people out.

So, when it comes to proof of your knowledge, go above and beyond. Use video when you can, and if possible, involve outside sources to validate your claims so it's not just coming from you.

Here are some quick ideas for you to display your knowledge better so you can build more authority and trust in your marketplace:

✓ Appearing as a guest on podcasts, magazines, or talk-shows that are well-respected and followed in your industry.

✓ Creating handbooks or guides talking about industry best practices.

✓ Pointing out common mistakes or shortfalls of your industry and making recommendations.

Secret #25: Provide Proof of Results

The quality of your work is very important. I'm sure you're talented at your craft. But if no one ever gets to see the quality of your work, how will they ever know the difference?

The issue a lot of contractors run into is they might have an eye for their specific trade, but not for marketing it properly. They don't take good pictures of their work. They don't do a good job of displaying testimonials. And they're not very consistent in documenting their journey daily.

Every job you complete is another opportunity to advertise your business.

The pictures you take of the job can be turned into an ad. The happy homeowner can become a glowing testimonial. And any issues you come across along the way and resolve can be documented on social media and transformed into a piece of content.

At *Savant Marketing Agency*, we encourage our clients to send pictures of their work to us on a monthly basis for social media content, so we can post numerous times per week on their behalf.

This is all proof to your audience that you're in the business of results.

On top of that, just the fact you're constantly updating your audience on all the work you're doing is proof you're in demand. The more in-demand and busier you seem, the better.

After all, everyone wants what they cannot have.

Here are some results-oriented posts I recommend you do on a consistent basis to affirm your results to your prospects:

✓ **Before/after pictures**. Remember we talked about transformations back in Step 2? The same applies here. Make it part of your process to document the beginning, middle and end of every project. Take high-quality, clear and bright pictures. For these purposes, you don't need a professional camera or photographer. Any smartphone with an HD camera will be fine. Once complete, post these transformations on your social media with a little summary of the job.

✓ **Customer testimonials.** If you get a new 5-star review on Google, HomeStars, Facebook, Houzz, or somewhere else … take a screenshot of it and post it on your social. Say a couple words about how grateful you are for your awesome clients. This goes a long way.

✓ **Your crew at work**. It's very important to take pictures of yourself or your crew on the job because it shows the people behind your company. This is proof you're real, that you have employees, and you aren't just someone using stock photos from the internet.

I recommend you do these types of posts every day for maximum results. If not, do them as often as possible. This is a long-term strategy—and over time, you will prove you're not just some fly-by-night contractor.

There's something to be said for consistently showing up every day.

Secret #26: Show Proof of Success

This one makes many people uncomfortable. Mostly because they struggle with recognizing their own success, let alone announcing it publicly. But this is an important step in building authority. After all, if you can't even recognize your own success, how can anyone else?

The concept is simple. People are attracted to success and repelled by failure. There's a deep psychological effect at play here. No one wants to work with someone who is on a downward spiral. They want to work with a company growing year after year. Why?

Because it's a signal to the prospect's brain you're in demand and people want you. They think, "Wow, looks like business is going really well for them. They must be making a lot of money. I bet they do really good work."

I know it sounds ridiculous when I say it like that, but it's true. This is basically the conversation going on in your prospect's mind at a subconscious level.

So, avoid talking about your failures, struggles or setbacks on social at all costs. Instead, show as much proof as you can that your business is growing, and so is your success.

No, I'm not asking you to be braggadocious, conceited or vain. I'm simply saying you must control the narrative of how your company is perceived online. You must consistently show evidence of your success.

After all, that's part of what good marketing is all about.

Here are some examples of the type of proof I'm talking about when it comes to showcasing your success:

✓ **You received an award.** Companies like Houzz give out awards all the time for best service or best work. Take every opportunity you can to show these off.

✓ **Your team is growing.** If you recently hired a new employee, make an announcement on social about it. The only reason why you're hiring would be that you're growing. Congratulate your new employee and welcome them to the team.

- ✓ **You invested in a new truck or piece of equipment.** The fact you are investing in your company and buying more equipment to better your service is proof you're growing. You wouldn't be doing so otherwise.

- ✓ **You hit a new company milestone.** If you had one of your best years in business, announce it. This doesn't have to come off as being braggy or in bad taste. Instead, congratulate your team and comment on how hard they've worked this year to earn it.

Secret #27: Do Social Remarketing

To make a real impact on social media, you must use Facebook and Instagram's paid advertising features. You can't just post for free all the time. Unfortunately, business pages don't get as much reach to followers as they used to.

So, you must make paid advertising part of your social media marketing strategy.

However, in our experience, using social media to advertise to a cold audience isn't very effective. Mostly because Facebook's algorithm only targets people based on their interests, which doesn't always signify buyer intention.

After all, just because you have an interest in bathroom renovations based on a Facebook page you liked, that doesn't mean you're looking for a renovation in the next month. We spoke about this briefly in Step 3, when I was explaining some of the advantages Google Ads has in that department.

However, social media *re*marketing is an essential tool for any contracting business. Why? Because these prospects have already interacted with your business in some capacity.

If you've been taking steps to action all the secrets in this book, you've already done 90% of the work to get people to your landing page using Google Ads. But for whatever reason, they weren't ready in that moment to take things further with your business.

This means we need to follow up with them virtually and continue to remind them of our offer. In this section, I'm going to break down at a high level how you can remarket to your previous website visitors via Facebook and Instagram:

In five steps, here's how to set up your remarketing campaign (for detailed instructions, check out https://www.facebook.com/business/help).

1. **Create a Facebook Business Manager account.** This is where you will be setting up your ads. (Do not use the standard "boosting" feature on your standard Facebook page–it's limited in capability.)

2. **Install a Facebook Pixel on your landing page.** The Facebook pixel is a small piece of code you insert on your landing page and thank you page (the page that automatically comes up when someone submits for a quote through your website). It tracks visitors and removes prospects who have already become leads.

3. **Create a custom audience**. Go into your Ads Manager and create a custom audience for your ad. Here, you're able to indicate you'd like to target people who've visited your landing page but didn't become a lead.

4. **Select relevant placements**. I recommend you place your ads in the Facebook and Instagram news feed. There are a couple of other options too. Use these too if you'd like but be mindful of your ad budget. Prioritize the news feed!

5. **Create your ad.** I recommend you create an ad from a post you've already made on your business page. Choose a before/after posting you did that got the MOST engagement compared to others. This validates it was successful and gets

people's attention. Now, simply add your landing page link in the call to action (CTA) and add a headline saying something like, "Request Your Free Quote."

ACTION STEPS

Get noticed and build authority using social media! Here's how to get started:

1. **Prove you know what you're talking about.** Use video when you can, and outside sources to validate your claims.
2. **Prove your business creates results.** Don't just say you get stuff done—*show* it by posting before-and-after pictures, customer testimonials, and photos and videos of your crew on the job.
3. **Prove you're a successful business.** If you've won an award or your company is growing, post about it.
4. **Social Remarketing.** Follow up with them using paid Facebook Ads and continue to remind them of your offer.

SUCCESS STORIES: PUTTING IT ALL TO WORK

Proven Case Studies That Break Down How We Implemented Our 7-Step Marketing Method For Our Clients!

As we come to the end of this book, you should have identified some things you need to act on—and started building a plan of action to grow your business.

Now, I want to encourage you this *stuff works*. I'm about to show you some additional case studies of how this has played out for other renovations, flooring, and landscaping businesses. Many times, we learn best from observing others in real-life examples of implementation.

The following stories are real case studies from clients we've worked with, outlining how we transformed their marketing and lead generation systems. Many of them have either *doubled, tripled, or even QUADRUPLED their revenues* since working with us.

Case Study #1: Matt Creamer Contracting Inc.

When we started working with them, the owner Matt Creamer was a new business. He worked as a subcontractor for many years as a carpenter, but then decided it was time to go out on his own.

Most of Matt's business relied on referrals. After a year of trying to drum up more business on his own, he decided he needed to put an aggressive plan in place to grow the business.

He connected with us, and we implemented the 7-Step Marketing Method I've outlined throughout the course of this book.

The first thing we did was create a niche for Matt and a USP. Since he'd been a carpenter for many years and most of his sales volume included decks and fences, we decided that would be his niche.

In only four months, Matt was able to generate over 200 qualified deck and fencing leads using a Google Ads campaign. He booked himself up for the entire season. In fact, he had to stop the campaign early because he hadn't anticipated the type of growth he ended up experiencing.

That four-month campaign brought in an additional $200k in revenue from just decking projects alone. Matt quadrupled his monthly sales.

Here's what Matt Creamer said: "Matt has taken my company from being a one-man show to now four full-time employees—and we're looking to hire more."

Case Study #2: Flooring Now

When Dave from Flooring Now came to us, he was frustrated with online marketing. He was already working with another marketing agency, but they weren't delivering on the promises they'd made.

In fact, they couldn't get him a single lead.

After walking him through our strategy and showing results we've gotten for clients like him, Dave decided to give our agency a shot.

His most profitable service within his business was floor refinishing. We defined that as his niche and created a comprehensive Google Ads campaign focused on keywords like "Floor Refinishing" and "Refinishing Hardwood Floors." We also advised him to take before/after pictures of his jobs, which we then posted on his social media.

Within a year, Dave increased his monthly revenue by 280%, and had also begun expanding his team.

Not only does Dave no longer have to worry about leads, but he can also continue to grow his team. According to Dave: "Things are going fantastic!"

Case Study #3: Magnolia Construction

Originally, Joey from Magnolia Construction didn't think he needed help growing his business. He ignored digital marketing for years because he wasn't tech savvy, until he realized his competitors were gaining an upper hand.

He contacted us to help him get up to speed with his online presence and implement a lead generation campaign—and niched himself into basement renovations.

Over the course of our initial six-month campaign, Joey was able to double his monthly revenue. He then reached a point where the infrastructure of his business could not support the growth he was having—and had to hire an estimator and even put a full management team in place to continue the steady and stable growth.

Joey has continued to invest more ad spend into his campaigns because he continues to make a profit from his monthly Google Ads campaigns.

Joey says, "Matt has grown my company exponentially!"

NEXT STEPS

Congratulations! I hope you've enjoyed going through *Digital Marketing Secrets for Contractors.* The 7-Step Marketing Method I've laid out for you is responsible for some amazing results, and I say that humbly.

Many of our clients have added multiple six figures to their bottom line and transformed their personal lives for the better because they invested their time, money, and resources into building a sustainable, profitable and scalable business that fuels their desired lifestyle.

And if you apply the teachings I've given you and follow them closely, I have no doubt you'll be equally as successful too.

Remember, if you get stuck along the way, refer back to this material as your main resource for guidance. This 7-step program is your roadmap to success. And you don't have to reinvent the wheel to make this work.

However, if you find yourself in the situation where you either don't have the time, resources, or patience to implement our 7-Step Marketing Method yourself …

I'd like to offer you a very special opportunity.

Our team at **_Savant Marketing Agency_** is happy to do all the heavy lifting for you: offering a 100% complete turn-key solution to build, implement, manage, and optimize all your marketing campaigns— month after month.

All you must do is promptly follow up with your leads, provide exceptional quality service to your new clients, and keep a close line of communication bi-weekly to ensure you're on the path to achieving your business goals. With our help, of course.

But here's the catch: we don't work with everyone.

Because of the high volume of contractors requesting our assistance, and because we're a relatively small boutique agency with limited capacity to take on more clients … spots are limited, and _very_ exclusive.

Here are the criteria for the businesses we work with:

1. You own a successful remodelling, flooring, or landscaping business
2. Your annual revenues are a minimum of $500K/year

3. We don't already have a client in your territory (yes, clients get exclusivity in their niche and city)

Oh, and above all, you must have a can-do attitude and a friendly demeanor! We have a very close relationship with all our clients and value strong relationships in business. So, it's important we get along on a personal level too.

If that works for you, and you'd like to learn more about how we might be able to help you implement our 7-Step Marketing Method …

Go to www.CallSavant.com and schedule your 100% free, no-obligation strategy call *today!*

During our 30-minute phone call together, we'll ask you some specific questions about your business—and define your personal goals and vision for your company.

Then, if we determine that we're a good fit for each other, we'll walk you through exactly how we will customize the 7-Step Marketing Method for your business—and explain what it would look like for us to work together and handle all your marketing needs.

Make sense? Great.

Talk soon my friend, I look forward to speaking with you.

Sincerely,

Matt Thibeau

P.S. Remember—if you'd like our team to create, implement, and manage all your marketing FOR you ... schedule your free call today. Hurry, because clients get exclusivity in their city and niche! Don't wait until your spot gets picked up by someone else and it's *too late*. Go to www.CallSavant.com now.

BONUS OFFER – *Download Your Free Audio Book*

Thank you so much for purchasing your copy of Digital Marketing Secrets for Contractors. If you are anything like me, you are much more of an auditory learner and always on the go. With that in mind, I have also recorded an audio version of this material so you can listen while you drive, work, eat or travel!

Go to www.SavantBook.com to gain instant access to your free audio version of this book now!

Manufactured by Amazon.ca
Bolton, ON

17577999R00072